Written by: Donesa Walker
Design by: Will Baten

Dedication

Hats are sometimes not a choice after we have been through certain seasons of our lives. I have watched so many of my sweet friends and family walk through trying times and earn their ultimate crown or final hat of this life. I dedicate this book to all those who went on before into eternity and embrace their examples of how to gracefully wear the hats we have been given whether they be seasons we enjoy or dread. The hat is only for a time, and I am thankful for this lesson from these graceful women and men in my life.

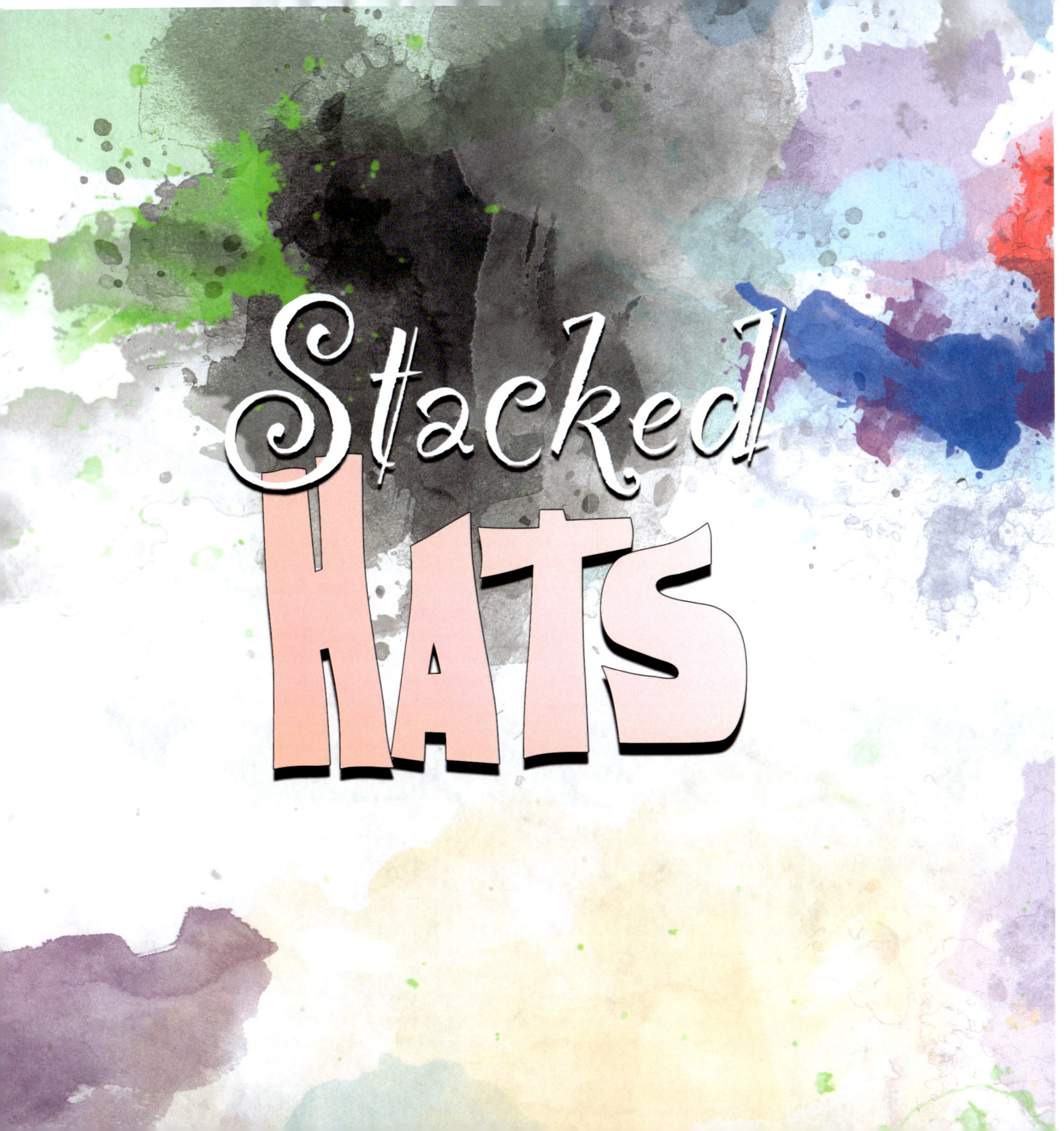
Stacked
HATS

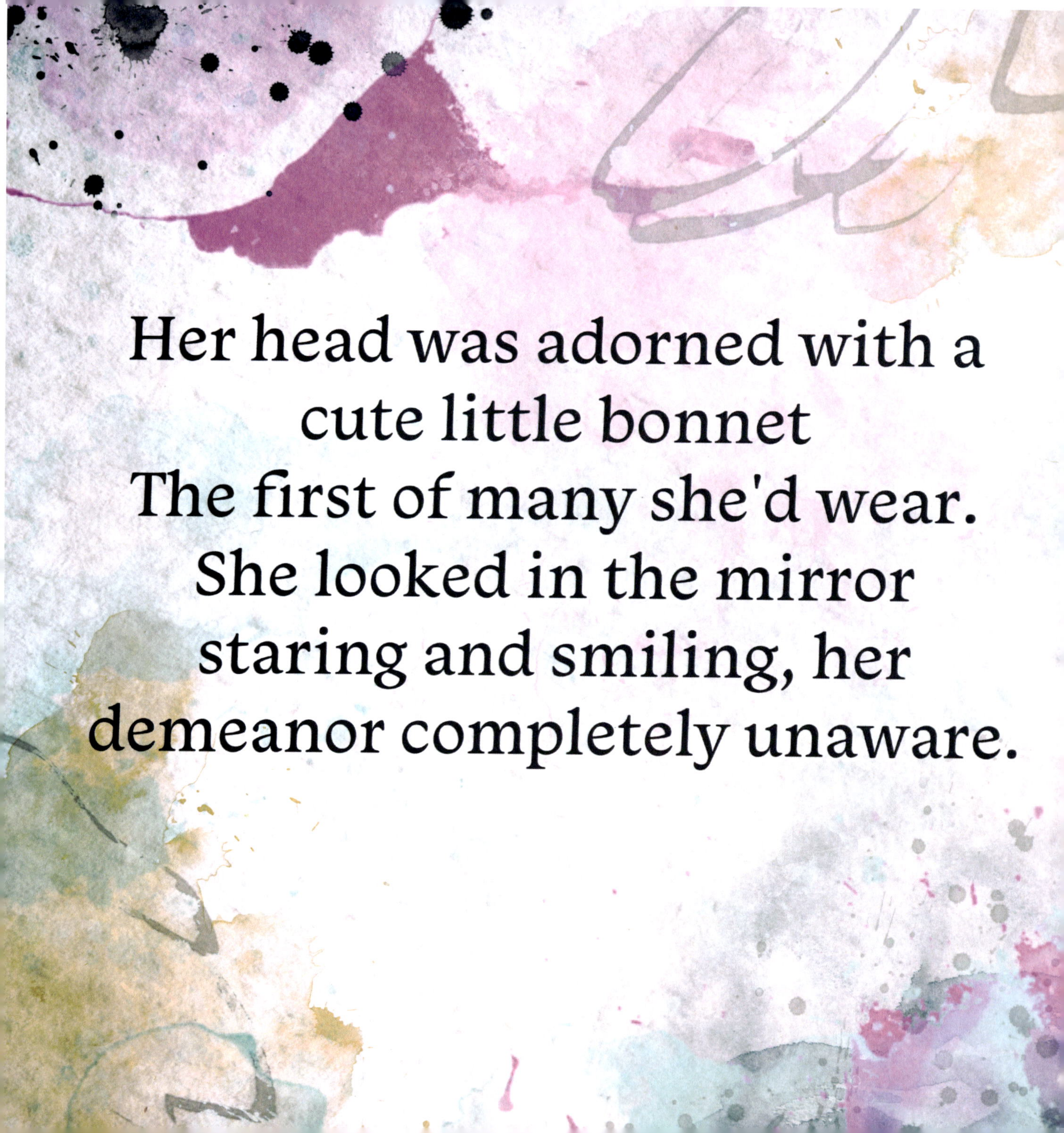
Her head was adorned with a
cute little bonnet
The first of many she'd wear.
She looked in the mirror
staring and smiling, her
demeanor completely unaware.

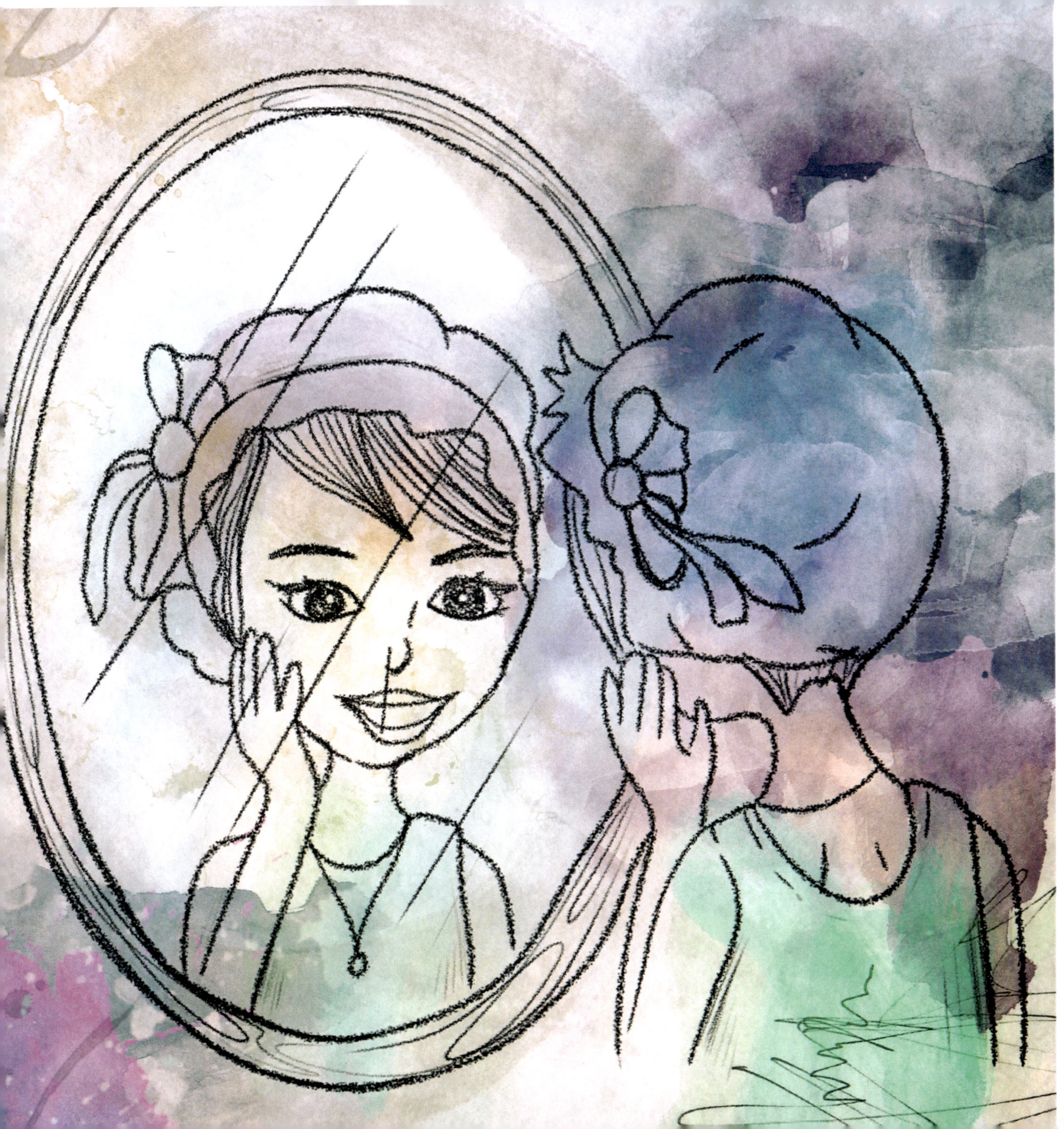

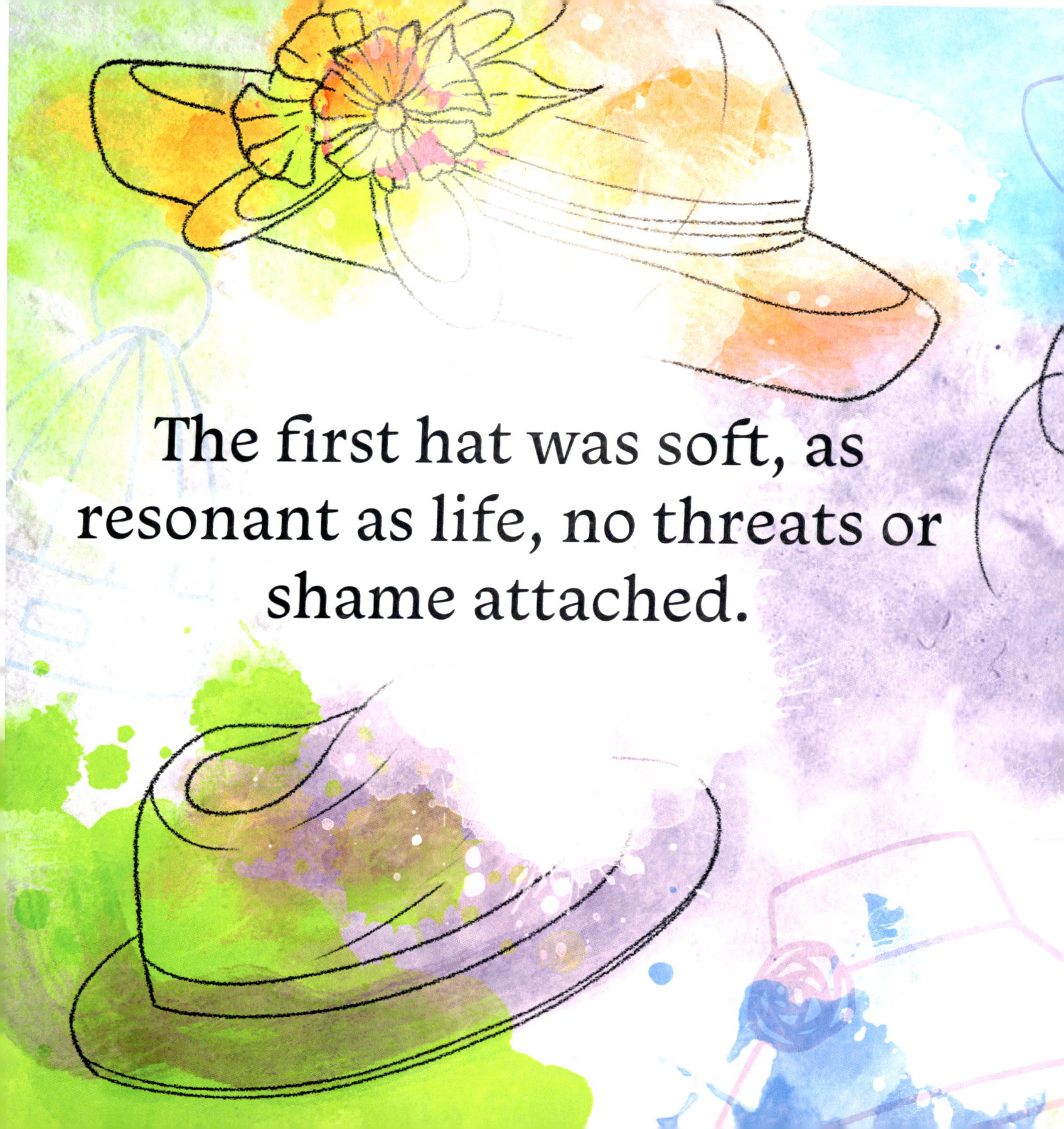
The first hat was soft, as resonant as life, no threats or shame attached.

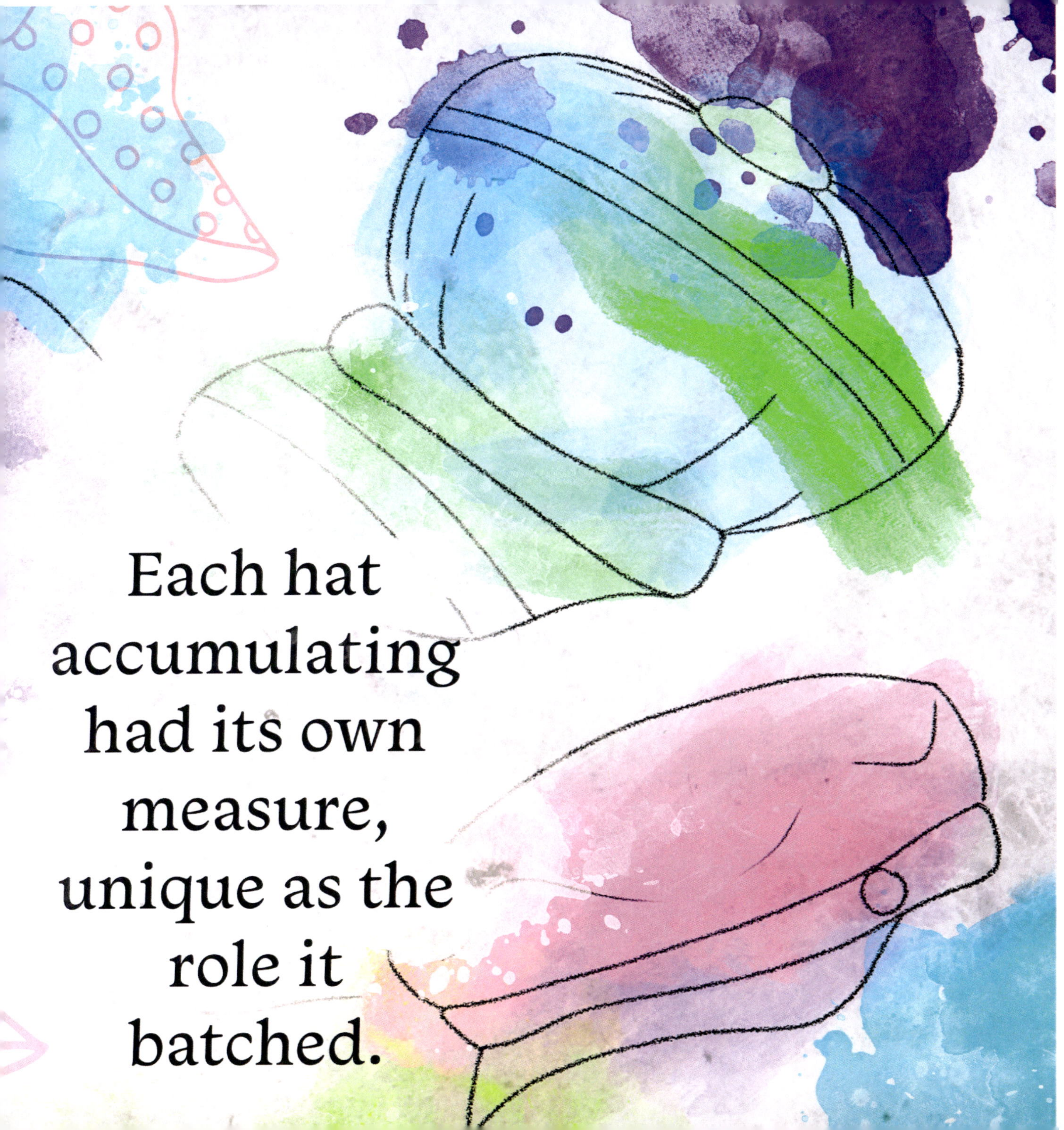

Each hat
accumulating
had its own
measure,
unique as the
role it
batched.

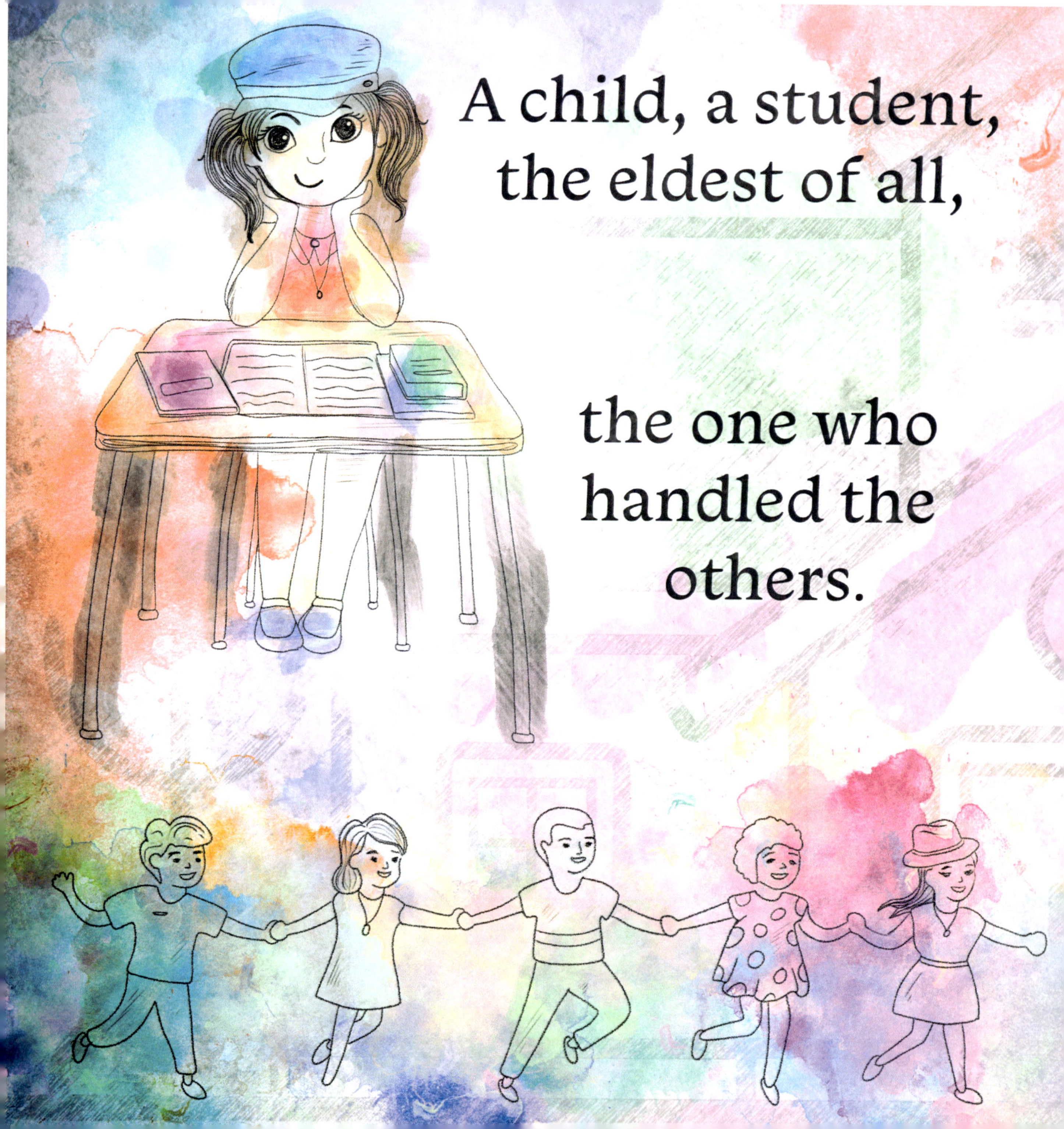

A child, a student,
the eldest of all,

the one who
handled the
others.

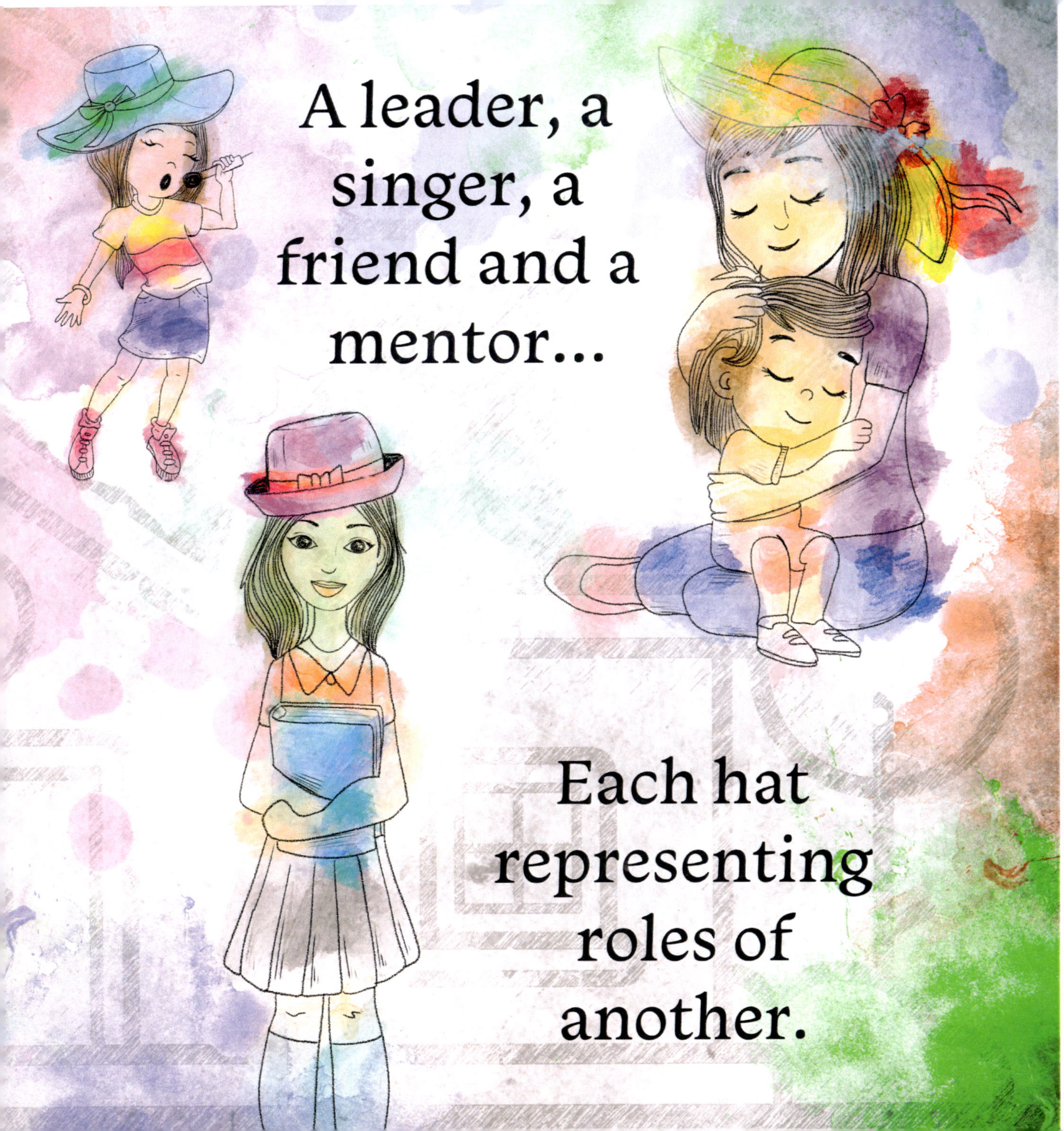

A leader, a singer, a friend and a mentor...

Each hat representing roles of another.

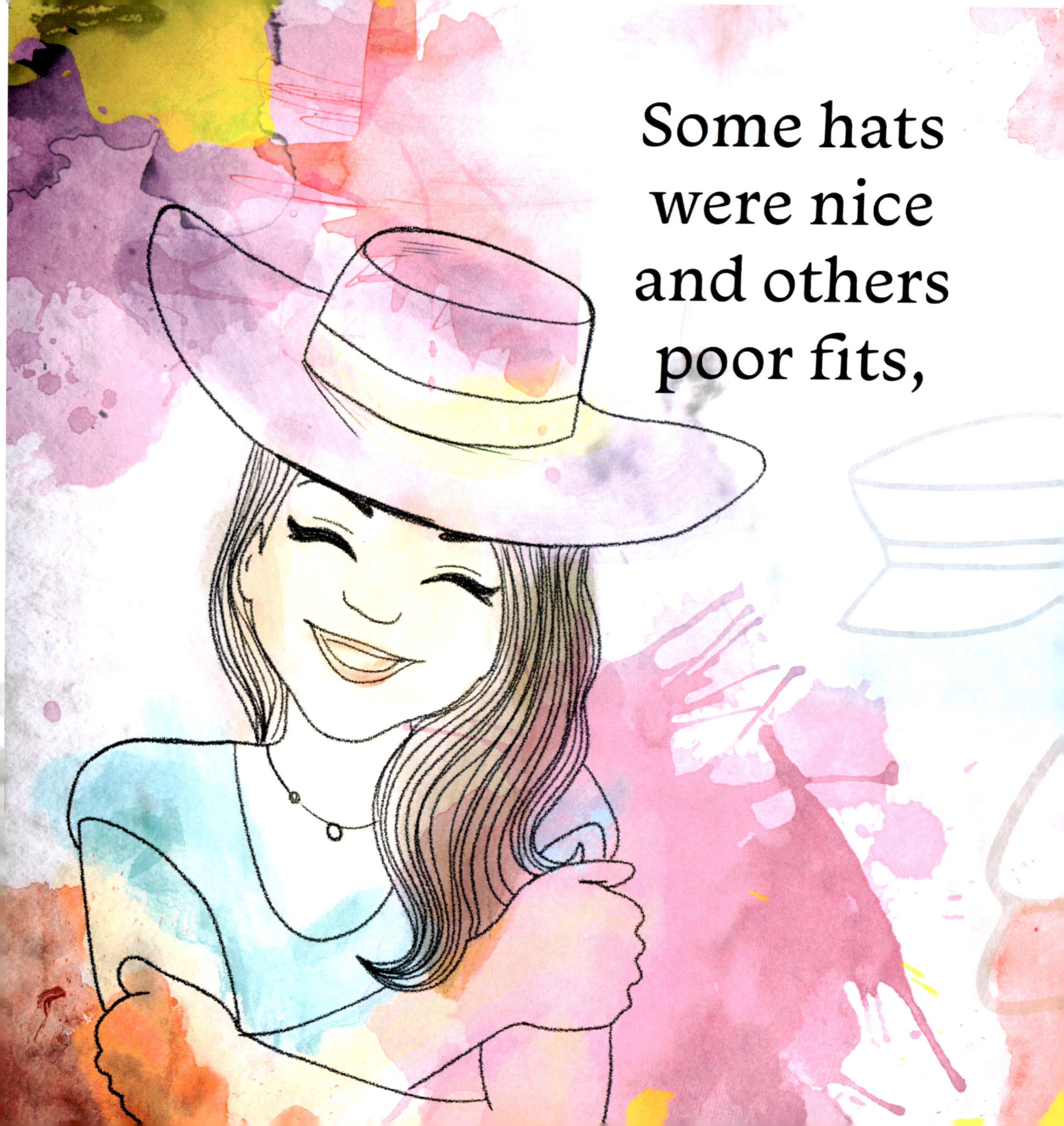
Some hats
were nice
and others
poor fits,

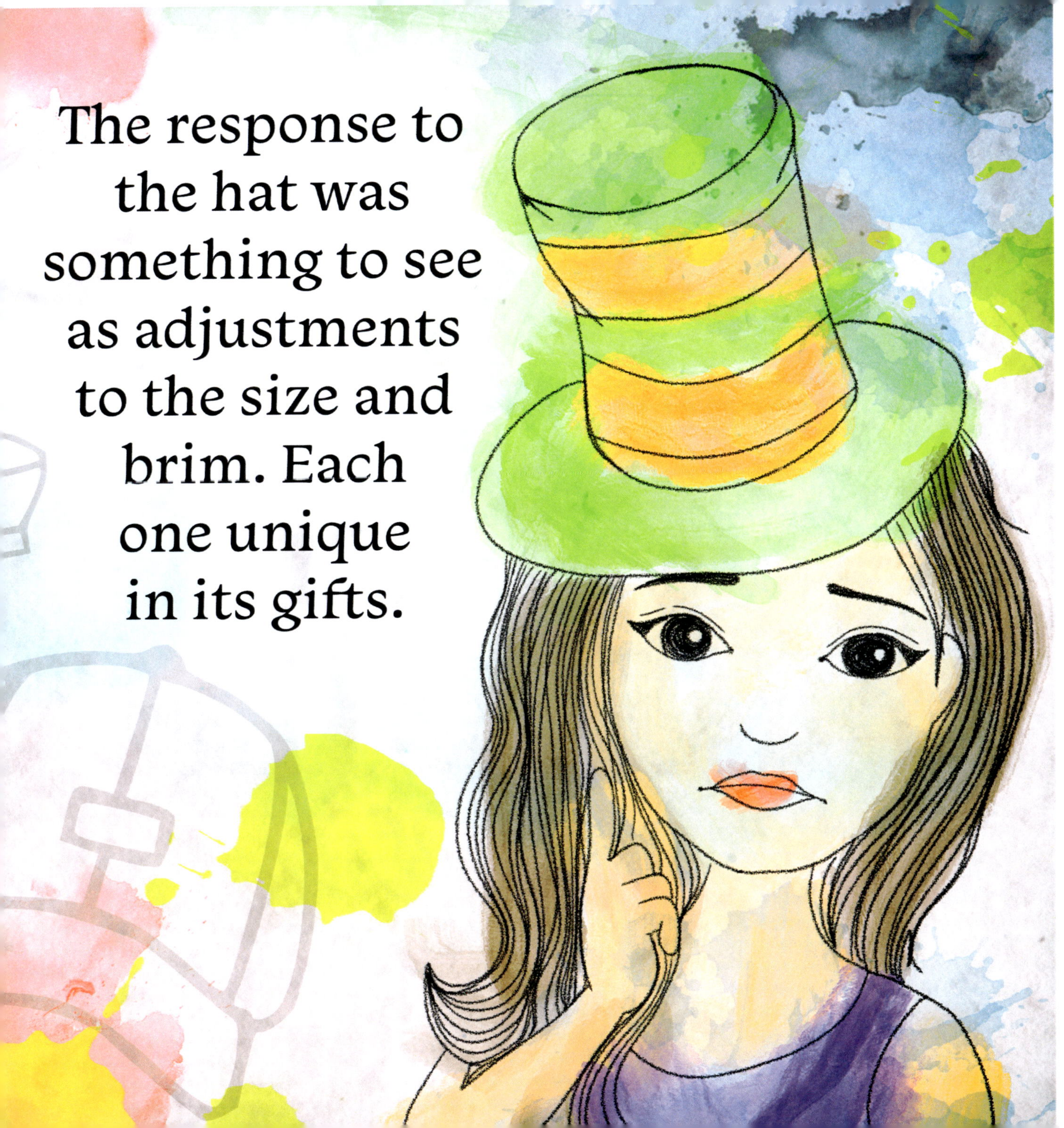
The response to
the hat was
something to see
as adjustments
to the size and
brim. Each
one unique
in its gifts.

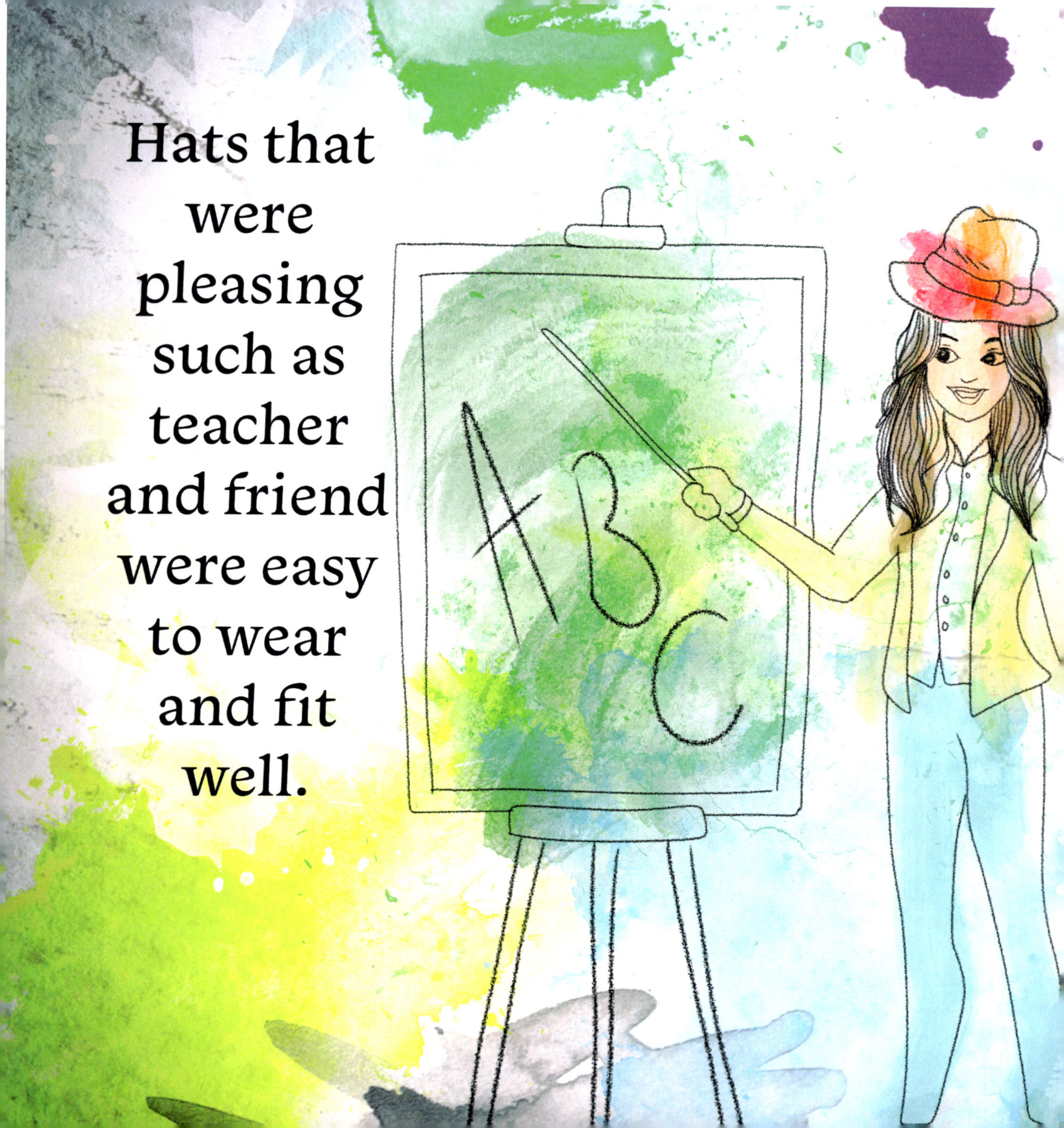

Hats that
were
pleasing
such as
teacher
and friend
were easy
to wear
and fit
well.

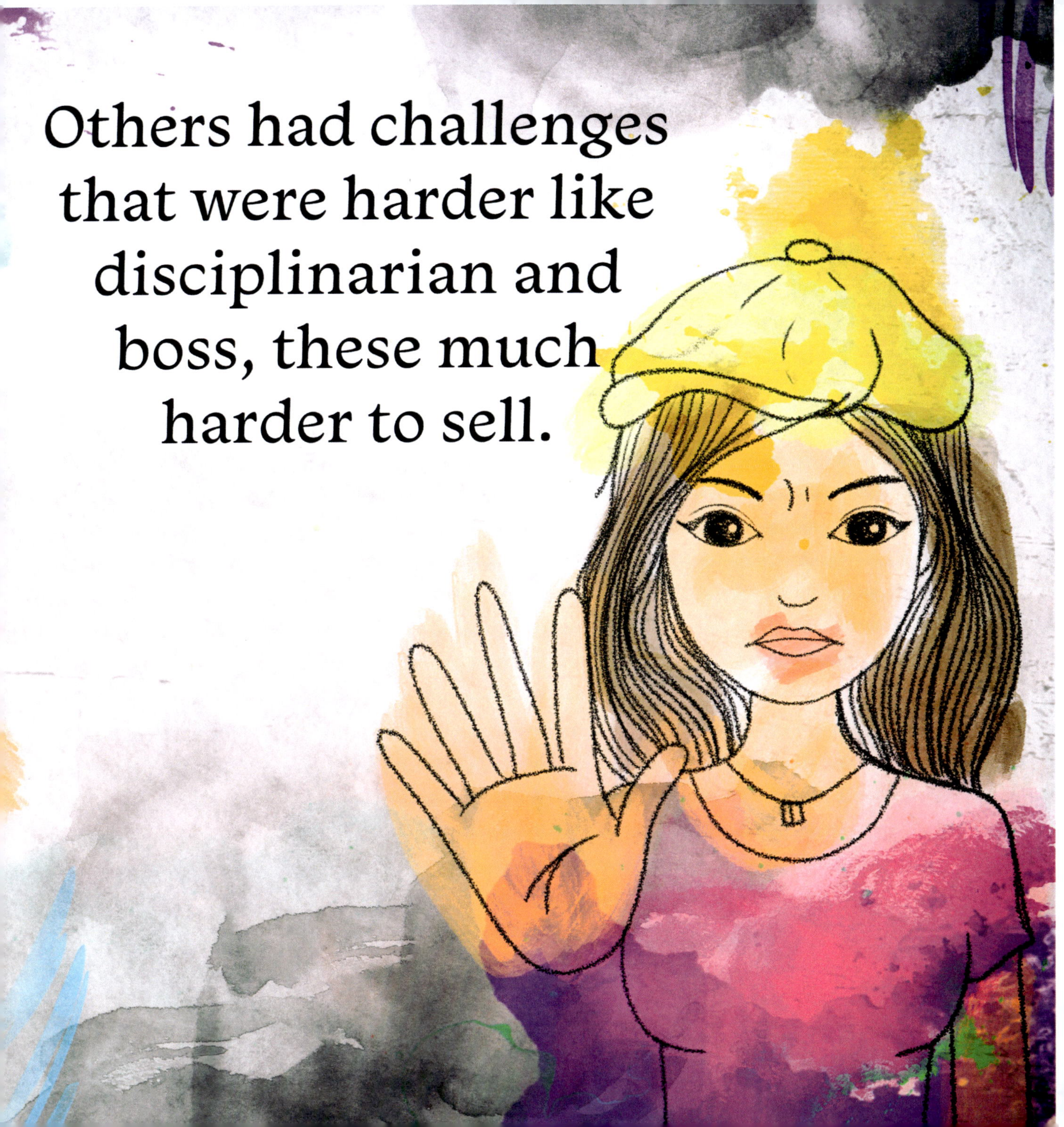
Others had challenges
that were harder like
disciplinarian and
boss, these much
harder to sell.

There were soft hats that grew, like wife and mother, their colors were bright and attractive then slowly would fade and become worn.

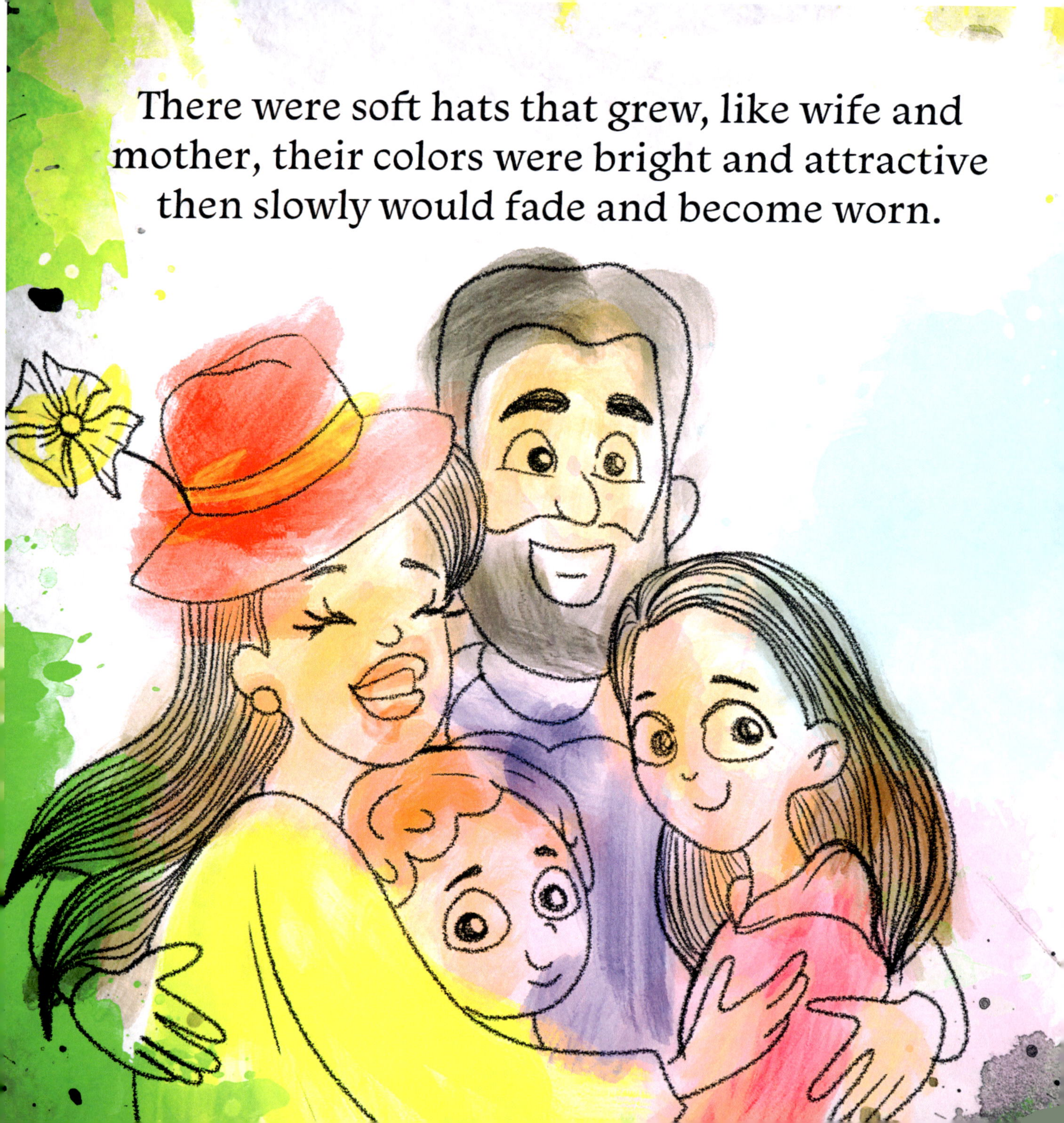

These hats were the cherished
that stood through time,
never would these be shorn.

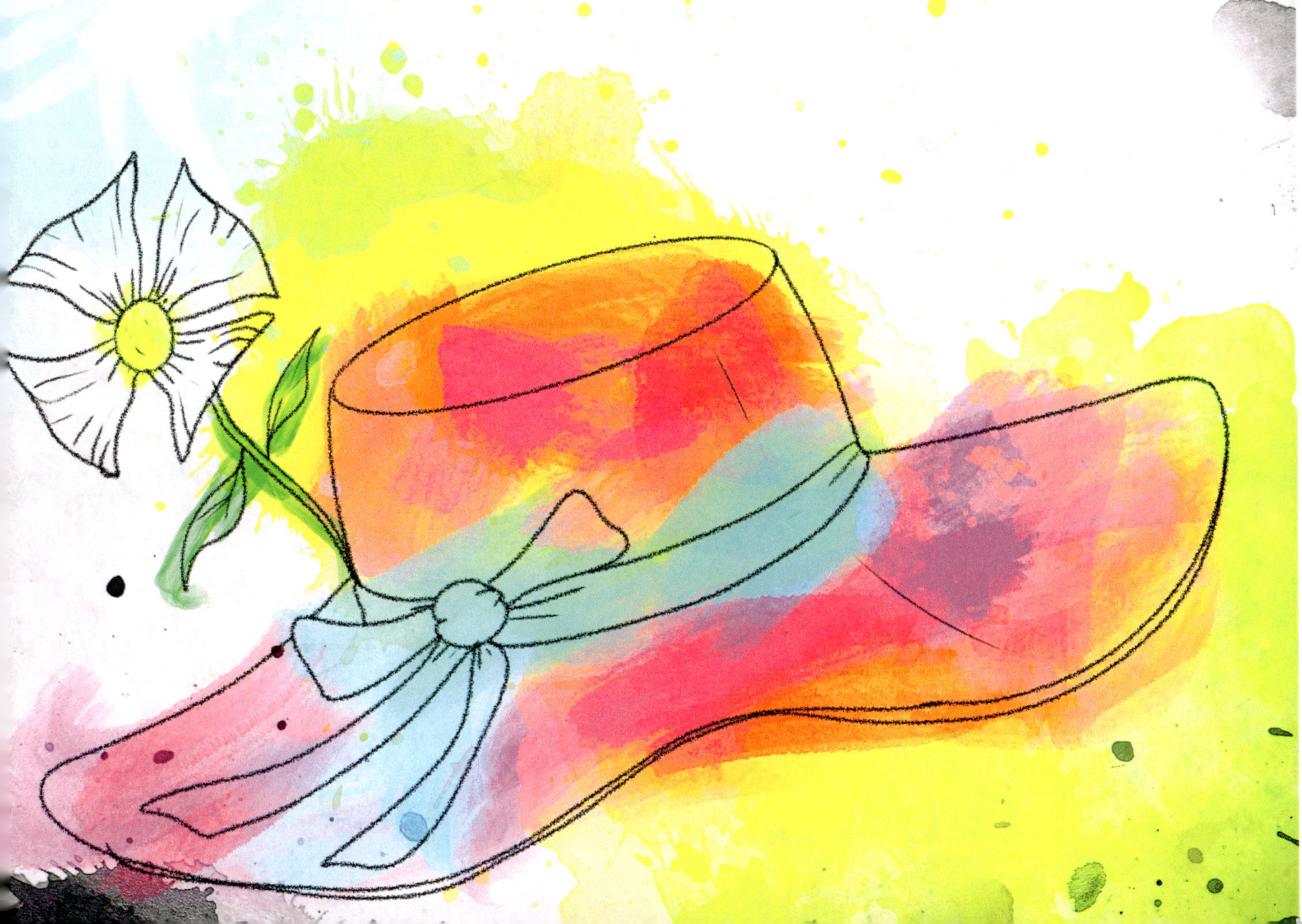

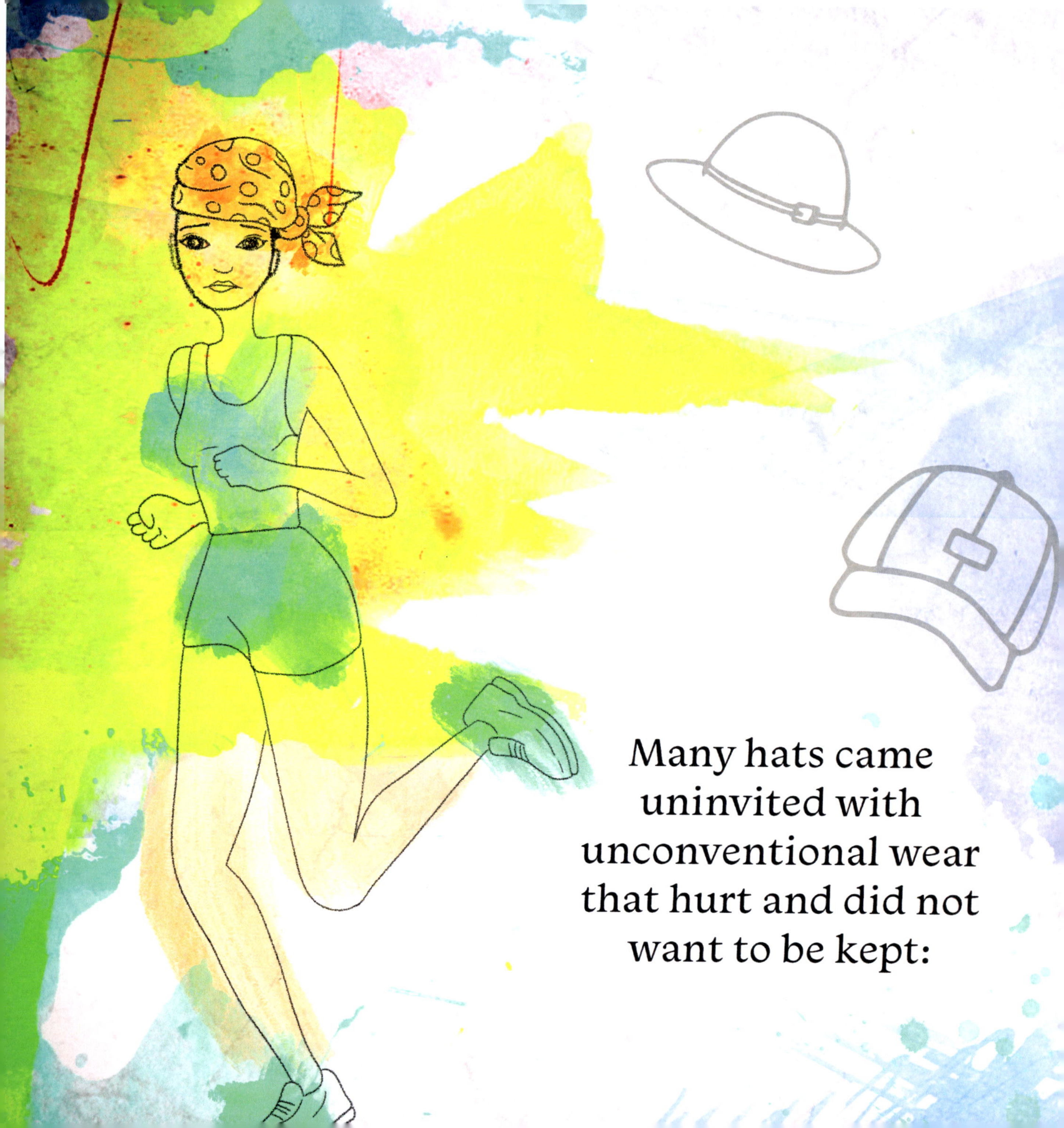

Many hats came
uninvited with
unconventional wear
that hurt and did not
want to be kept:

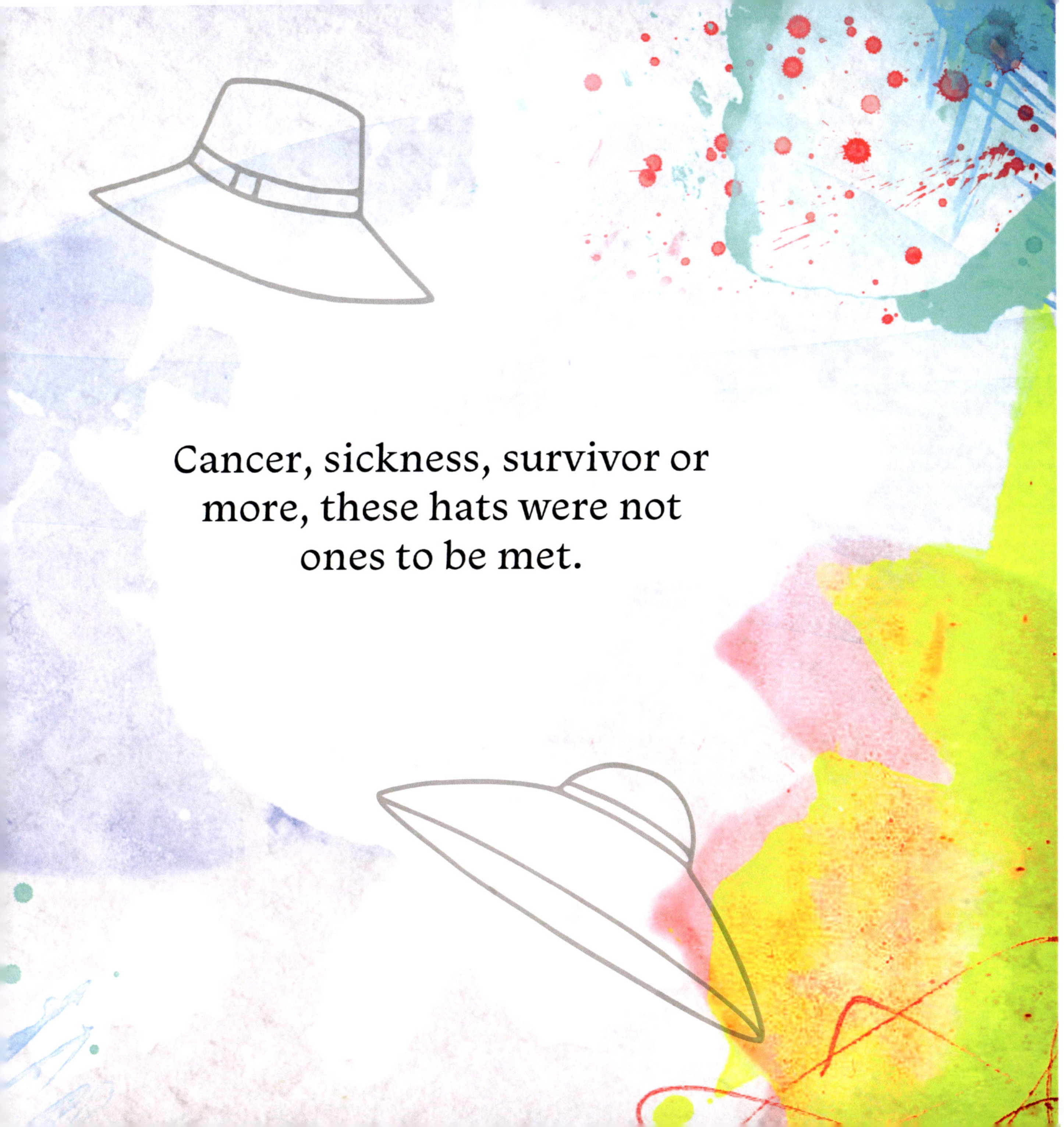

Cancer, sickness, survivor or
more, these hats were not
ones to be met.

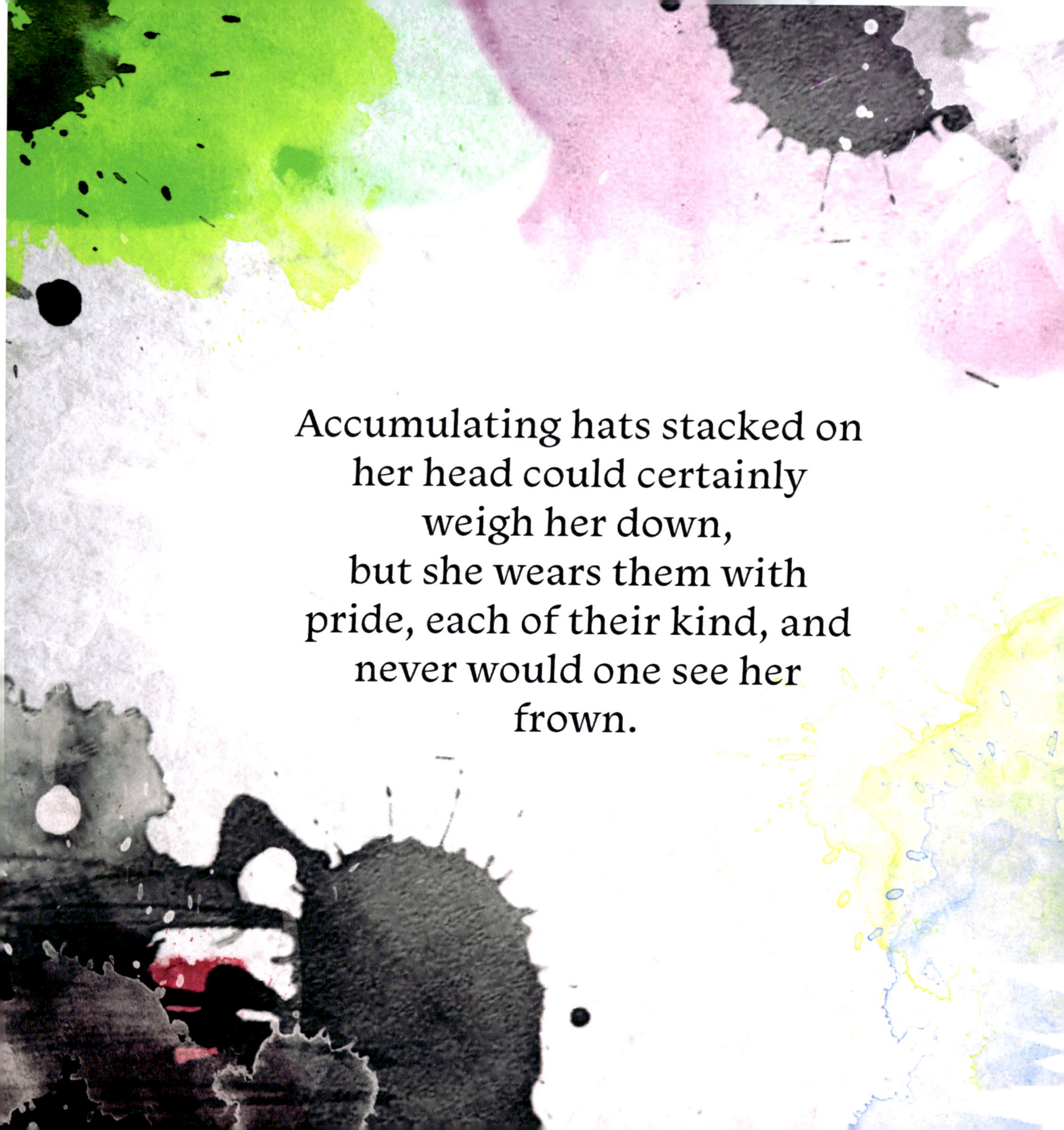

Accumulating hats stacked on
her head could certainly
weigh her down,
but she wears them with
pride, each of their kind, and
never would one see her
frown.

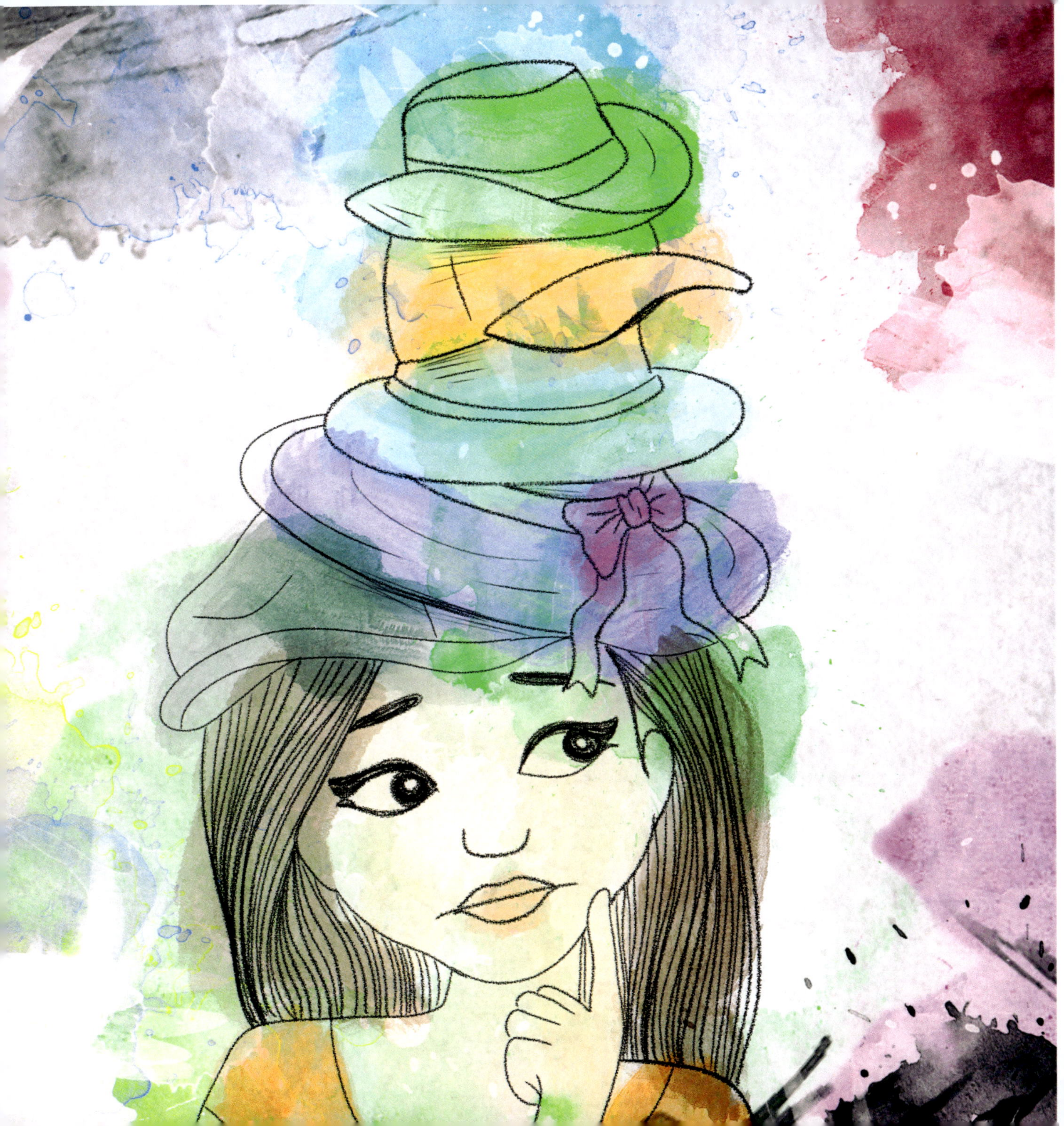

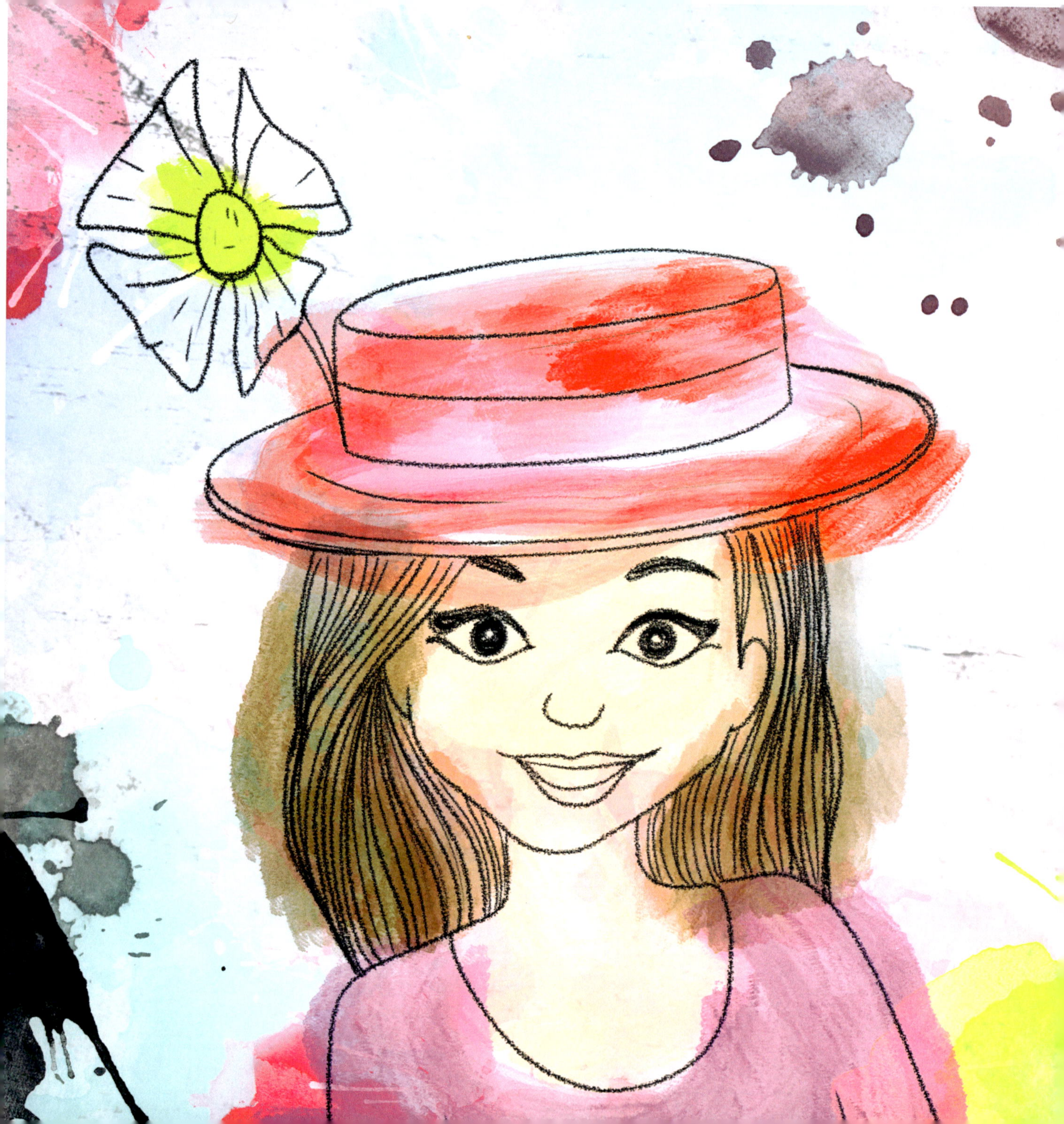

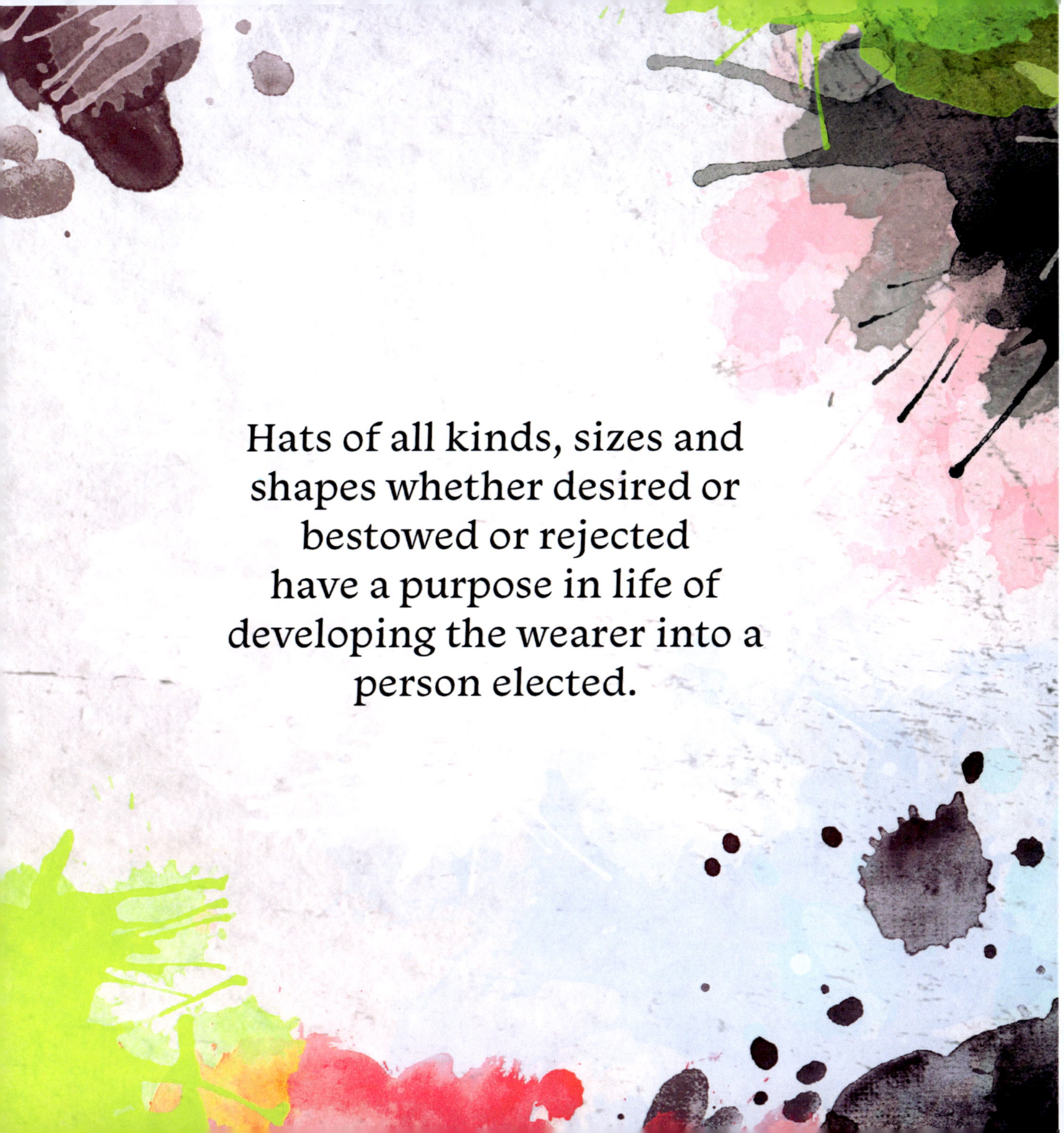

Hats of all kinds, sizes and
shapes whether desired or
bestowed or rejected
have a purpose in life of
developing the wearer into a
person elected.

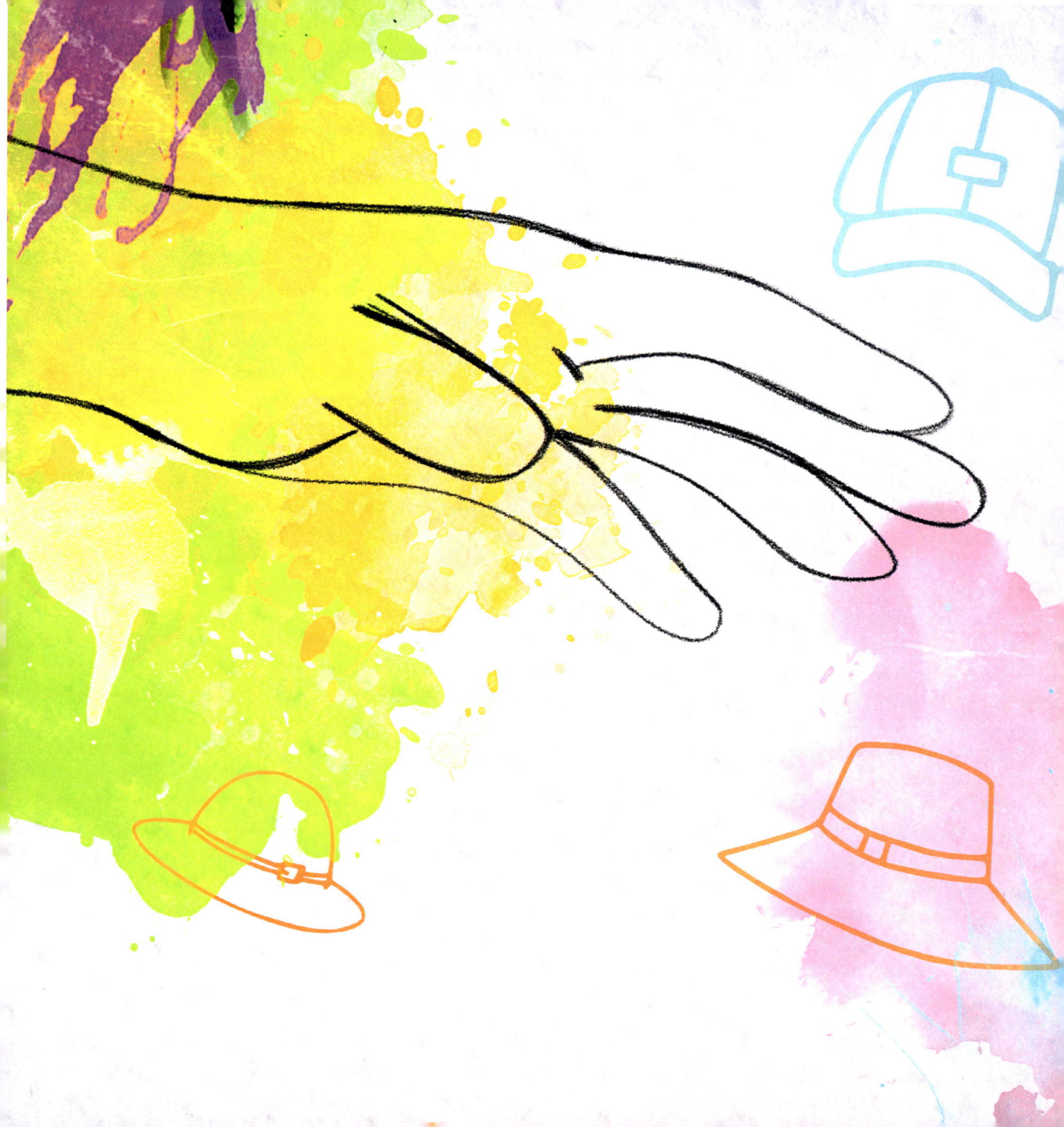

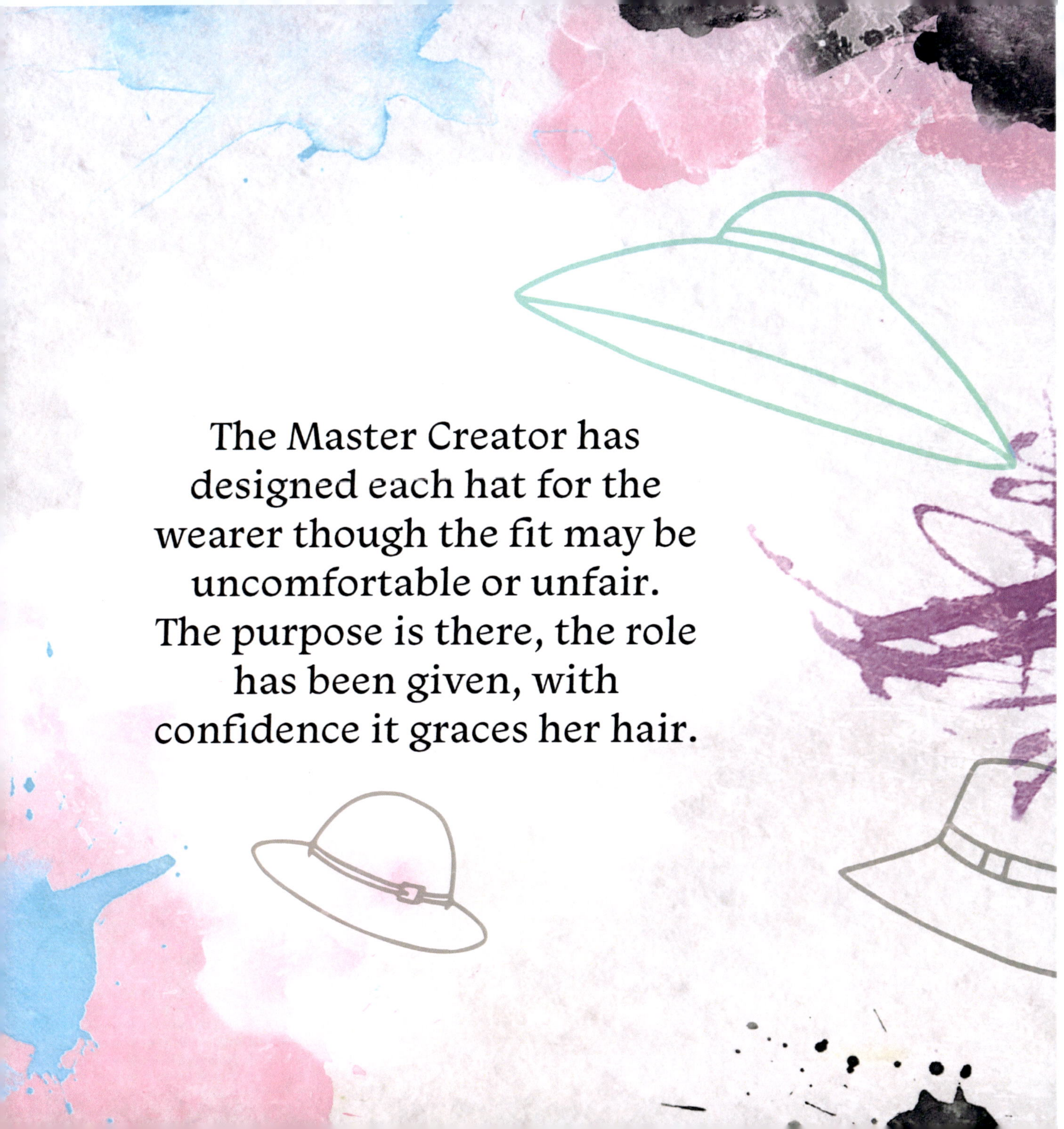

The Master Creator has
designed each hat for the
wearer though the fit may be
uncomfortable or unfair.
The purpose is there, the role
has been given, with
confidence it graces her hair.

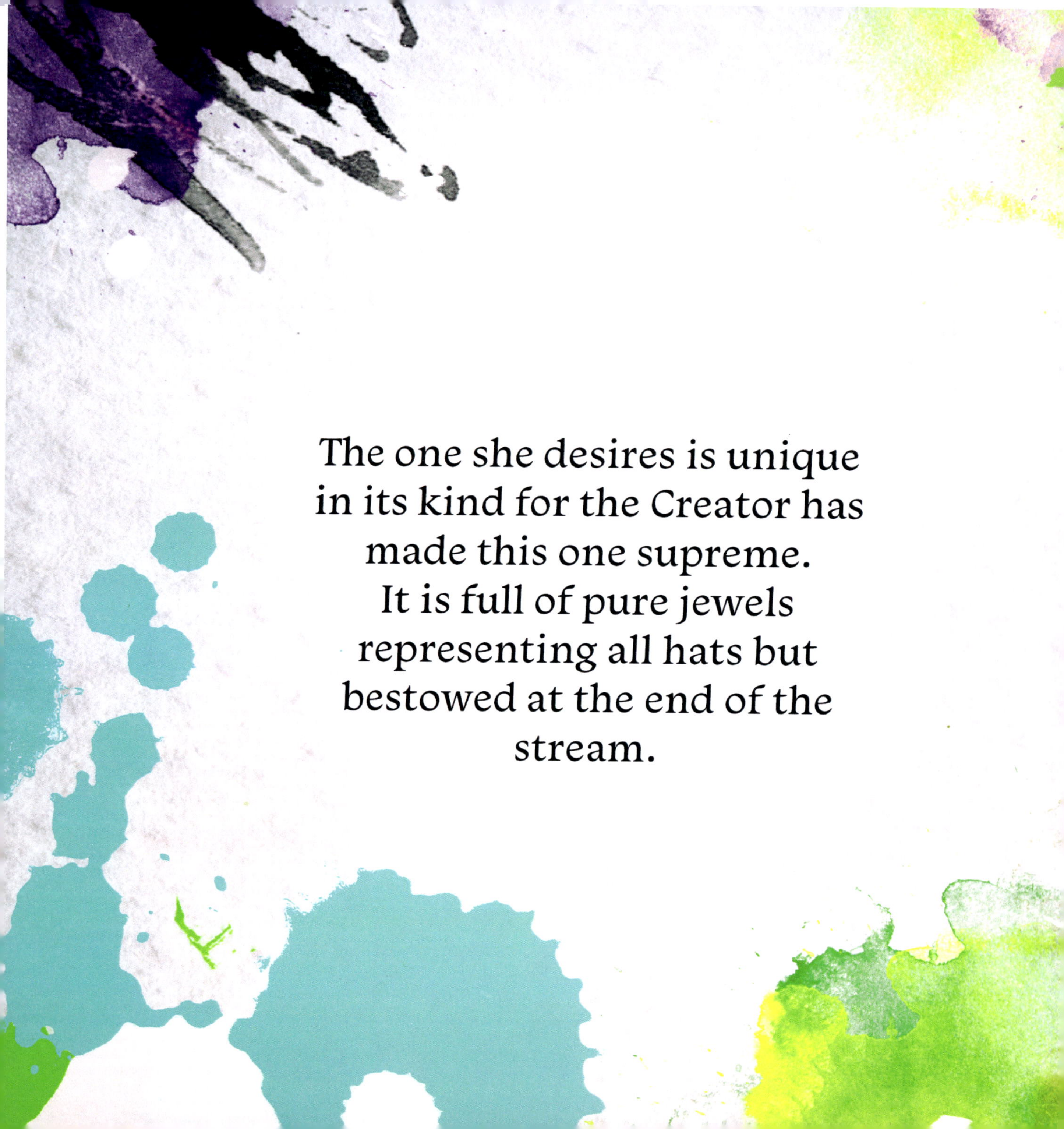

The one she desires is unique
in its kind for the Creator has
made this one supreme.
It is full of pure jewels
representing all hats but
bestowed at the end of the
stream.

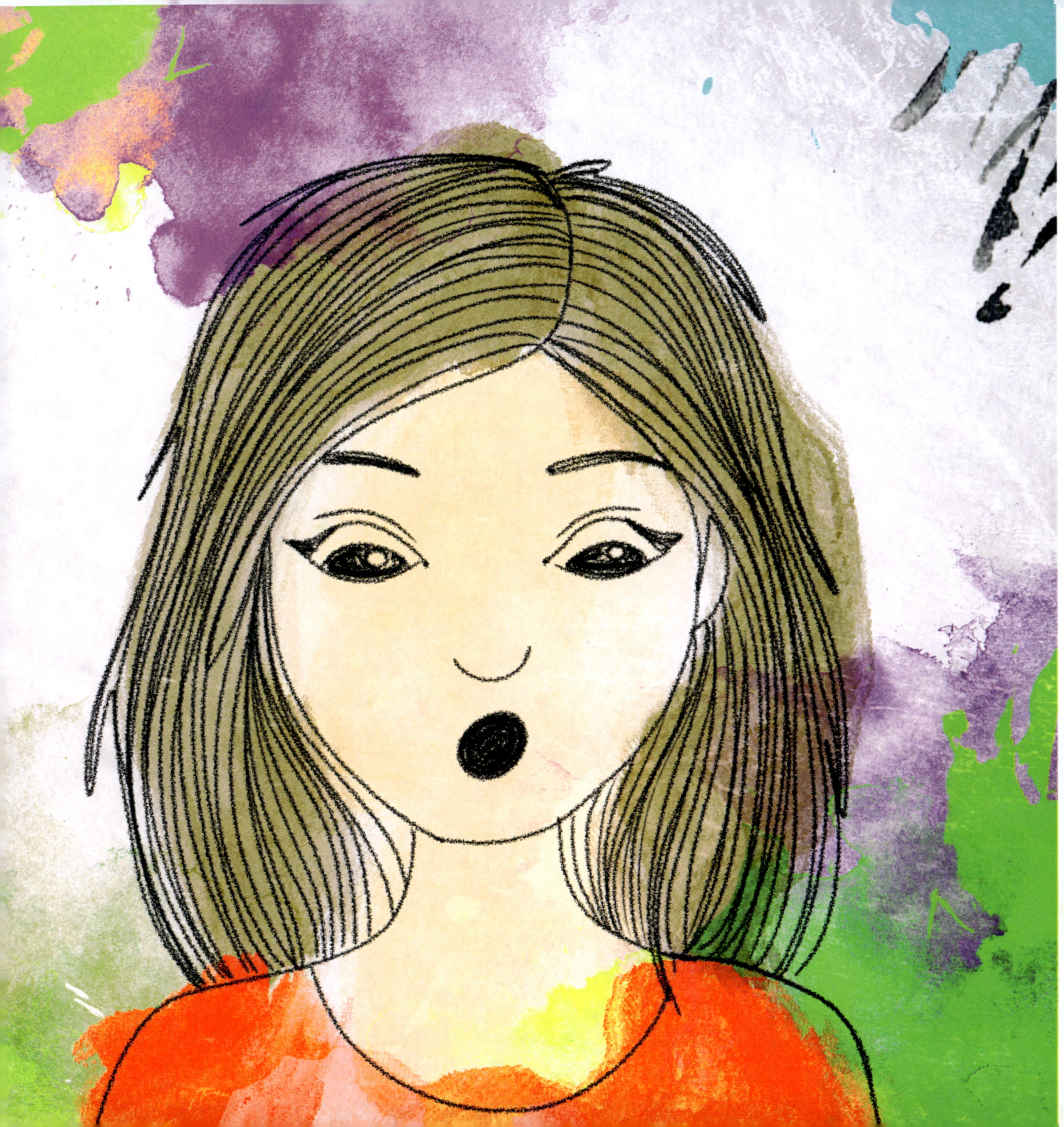

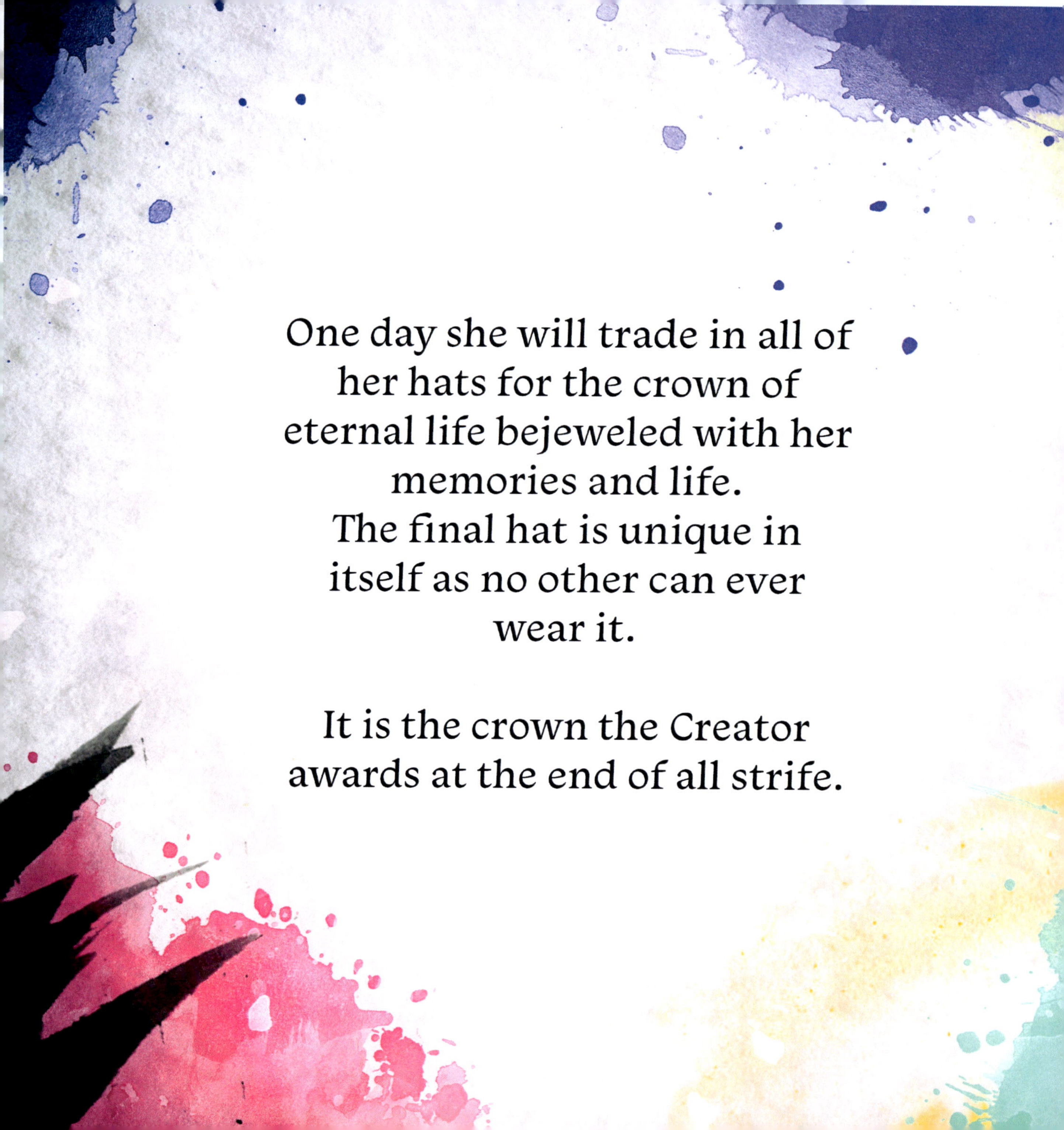

One day she will trade in all of
her hats for the crown of
eternal life bejeweled with her
memories and life.
The final hat is unique in
itself as no other can ever
wear it.

It is the crown the Creator
awards at the end of all strife.

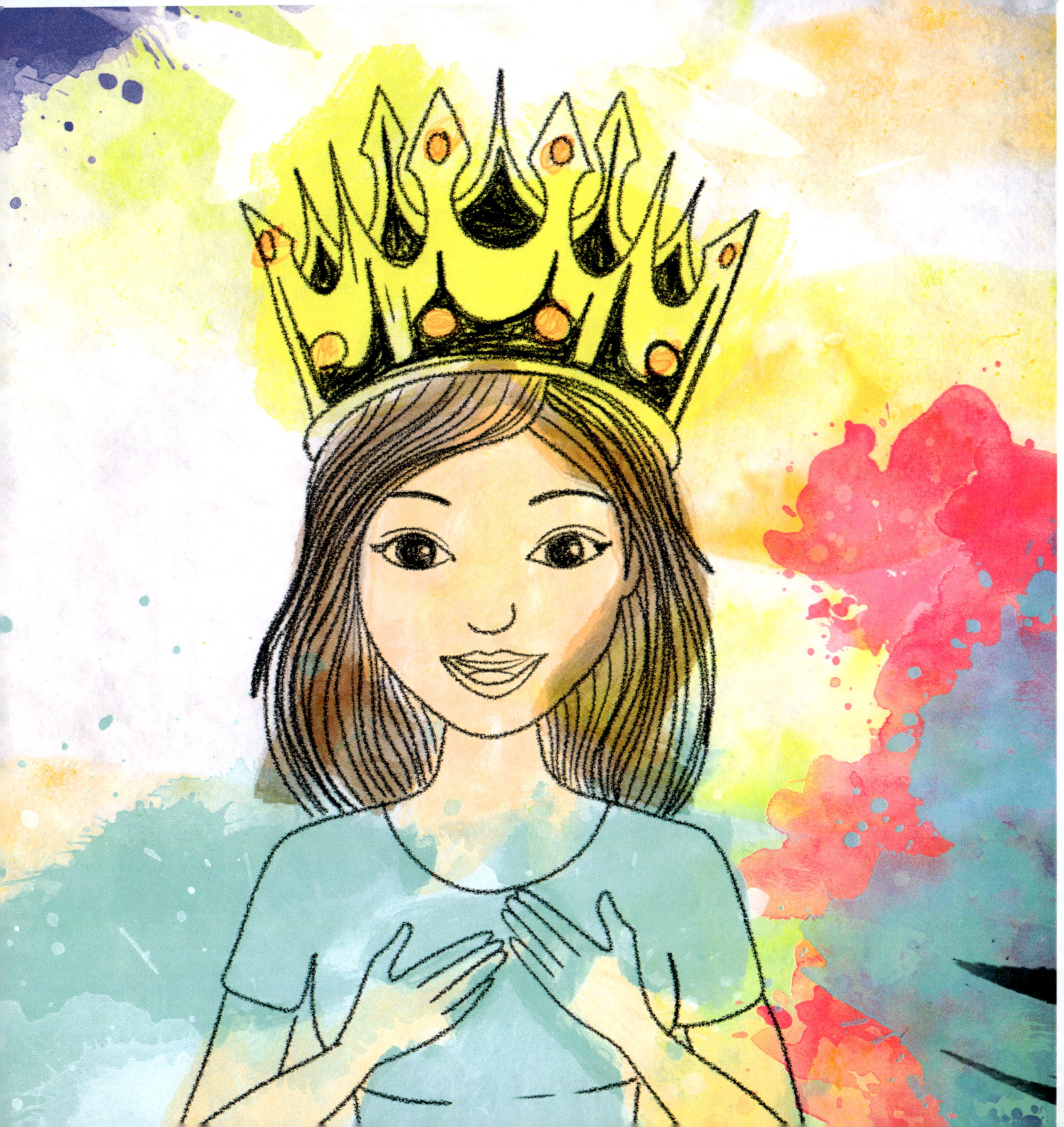

The End